ENTER THE DOJO!
MARTIAL ARTS FOR KIDS

BRAZILIAN JUJITSU

JASON BRAINARD

PowerKiDS
press
New York

Published in 2020 by The Rosen Publishing Group, Inc.
29 East 21st Street, New York, NY 10010

First Edition

Editor: Greg Roza
Book Design: Reann Nye

Photo Credits: Series art Reinhold Leitner/Shutterstock.com; cover, p. 10 guruXOX/Shutterstock.com; p. 5Marco Crupi/Shutterstock.com; p. 7 EVAN HURD PHOTOGRAPHY/ Sygma/Getty Images; p. 9 Holly Stein/Getty Images Sport/Getty Images; p. 11 Miljan Zivkovic/Shutterstock.com; p. 12 G-Force Vision/Shutterstock.com; p. 13 Pepsco Studio/Shutterstock.com; p. 14 Brandon Magnus/Zuffa LLC/UFC/ Getty Images; p. 17 Nomad_Soul/Shutterstock.com; p. 19 kali9/E+/Getty Images; p. 21 Nicola Tree/ Taxi/Getty Images Plus/Getty Images; p. 22 Vitalij SovaiStock/Getty Images Plus/Getty Images.

Cataloging-in-Publication Data

Names: Brainard, Jason.
Title: Brazilian jiujitsu / Jason Brainard.
Description: New York : PowerKids Press, 2020. | Series: Enter the dojo! martial arts for kids | Includes glossary and index.
Identifiers: ISBN 9781725310025 (pbk.) | ISBN 9781725310049 (library bound) | ISBN 9781725310032 (6 pack)
Subjects: LCSH: Jiu-jitsu–Brazil–Juvenile literature.
Classification: LCC GV1114.B73 2020 | DDC 796.8152–dc23

Manufactured in the United States of America

The activities discussed and displayed in this book can cause serious injury when attempted by someone who is untrained in the martial arts. Never try to replicate the techniques in this book without the supervision of a trained martial arts instructor.

CPSIA Compliance Information: Batch #CWPK20. For Further Information contact Rosen Publishing, New York, New York at 1-800-237-9932.

CONTENTS

Ready, Steady, Go!

Brazilian jujitsu is often called BJJ. It's a martial art. BJJ is also a popular sport. No weapons are used in BJJ. It focuses on ground fighting. This is called grappling. When on the ground, **opponents** use joint locks and choke holds to make their opponent "tap out," or **submit**. Locks and chokes are known as "submission" moves.

BJJ can keep you fit. It can also be used for self-defense. Using BJJ, a smaller fighter can beat a bigger and stronger opponent. This is one of the reasons it has become such a popular sport. It's also a lot of fun!

Kiai!

Brazilian jujitsu is a style of ground fighting. It's similar to wrestling in many ways. Both are grappling sports.

Brazilian jujitsu can look scary. It's actually a very safe sport when the opponents respect each other.

From Japan to a New World

In 1917, Japanese judo master Mitsuyo Maeda moved to Brazil, where he put on judo **demonstrations**. He inspired 14-year-old Carlos Gracie to begin studying judo and jujitsu. Carlos quickly became very good at them and opened his own school.

Carlos's brothers joined him as teachers. The youngest Gracie brother, Helio, was small and weak. Carlos would not let him train or teach at first. Instead, Helio watched and learned. Because of his small size, he found learning some judo moves very hard. This is when he began mixing elements of judo with jujitsu. This is how Brazilian jujitsu got its start.

Kiai!

The Gracies were so sure about BJJ that they invited martial artists from all over the world to participate in a sport they called *Vale Tudo*, or "anything goes" fighting. This led to the creation of modern mixed martial arts (MMA) **competitions**.

Not only did Helio become a master teacher in BJJ, he became one of its greatest champions. His favorite finishing move was the cross choke, which includes using the opponent's uniform to choke them.

Going Pro

In 1989, Helio Gracie's son Rorion opened the first Gracie Jiu-Jitsu Academy in Torrance, California. This helped make BJJ more popular in the United States.

In 1993, Rorion and some others started the Ultimate Fighting Championship (UFC) MMA competition. That year at UFC 1, Royce Gracie won three matches against larger opponents who were experts in karate and boxing. Martial artists who didn't know about BJJ were stunned. Royce's early success in UFC made people around the world take notice. Today, most mixed martial artists need at least a basic understanding of BJJ in order to compete at the highest levels.

All three wins Royce scored at UFC 1 were submissions. This showed the world how effective BJJ can be.

9

Takedowns and Mounts

Brazilian jujitsu matches begin with opponents standing and facing each other. They use judo and jujitsu throws to try to take each other to the ground.

Kiai!

Sweeps are moves used to transition, or move, from one mount to another. They can be used to get out from under a mount, or get out of an opponent's guard position. Sweeps show how a smaller person can gain control of a larger person in BJJ.

GUARD POSITION

Once on the ground, both fighters struggle for **dominance**. This is done by using different mounts. A full mount is when a person straddles their opponent's chest, and it's a very strong position. In a side mount, the person lies across their opponent's body. Another important skill is using the guard position. This is when the competitor on the ground wraps their legs around the person on top. This keeps the top fighter from getting more control over the bottom fighter.

Joint Locks

BJJ matches end when one of the competitors forces the other to tap out. This often happens because of a joint lock. Locks can be used on any of the body's joints, such as the wrists, elbows, and shoulders. These moves **hyperextend** a joint, which causes pain. They can also cause injuries when competitors aren't careful and respectful of each other. Popular locks include the arm bar, wrist lock, and the banana split!

Kiai!

It's very important to tap out if you can't get out of a joint lock. It's better to lose a match than to suffer an injury.

The arm bar is one of the most used locks in BJJ. It's a finishing move that often makes an opponent tap out quickly.

Many competitions ban the use of some locks on knees, ankles, and the spine. Bans on these locks help keep BJJ one of the safest full-contact sports.

13

Choke Holds

Choke holds are another type of move used to submit an opponent. Chokes cut off an opponent's air supply! It's very important to tap out if an opponent gets a choke hold on you.

Kiai!

A fighter placed in a choke hold might actually pass out for a few seconds if they choose not to tap out! BJJ students learn when to give up to protect their own health.

TRIANGLE CHOKE

Many chokes are sneaky and can be used by a smaller fighter on their back to beat a larger opponent on top of them.

When applying a cross collar choke—a favorite of Helio Gracie—you wrap part of your opponent's uniform around their neck and squeeze. Another common choke seen in MMA matches is the triangle choke. The competitor on the bottom lifts their leg up and over their opponent's neck, and then locks it in place with the other leg. Once applied, the triangle choke almost always ends the match.

How to Start

Finding a dojo that teaches Brazilian jujitsu isn't hard. Do some research before spending a lot of time and money. Read reviews online. Most places offer at least one free class to new students. Ask other students how they feel about their progress. Many karate dojos are mixed martial arts schools that also teach BJJ.

BJJ takes time to learn. Before learning chokes and locks, you will need to learn how to stay safe on the mat. New students are not allowed to **spar** standing up. They need to learn throws, mounts, and sweeps first. They also learn how to fall without getting hurt.

Kiai!

BJJ students learn a series of basic warm-up exercises that copy movements needed during a real match. These exercises can be tiring, but they help build **stamina** while learning **technique**.

Many BJJ students wear a uniform called a gi. Some dojos don't require students to wear gis.

17

Body and Mind

At first, BJJ may seem very hard. Instructors keep students moving all the time! Stick with it. As you learn, your fitness will improve. You will learn how to breathe properly and **conserve** your energy, allowing you to perform a surprising sweep or submission move. Your strength will increase, and so will your **flexibility**. These physical traits are important for BJJ competitors.

Brazilian jujitsu is also good for your mind. Competitors need to think several moves ahead in order to perform a throw, joint lock, or choke hold. As you improve, so will your memory and mental quickness.

Kiai!

Maybe you already know somebody who has been learning Brazilian jujitsu. It may be hard to think that you'll ever be as good as them. Don't worry! BJJ classes often have students of many different shapes, sizes, and ages, but they all have at least one thing in common. They want to learn BJJ!

A great thing about BJJ is that you learn at your own pace. It doesn't matter how young or old you are. What matters is the effort you put into it.

19

Rank

Like many martial arts, Brazilian jujitsu uses different colored belts to show what level a student has reached. There are fewer belts in BJJ than in other martial arts. These belts include white (for beginners), blue, purple, brown, and black. The greatest BJJ masters in the world wear red belts.

Students need to perfect new moves before moving up to their next belt color. They also must be respectful and not skip classes. Students need to stay fit and exercise. They may also be asked to help students of lower ranks. Sparring with students of a higher rank can sometimes be **frustrating**. Advancing in BJJ takes **commitment**.

Students may also earn stripes on their belts. This shows that they've reached smaller levels of success between belts.

21

Fights, Fitness, and Fun

There are numerous BJJ competitions each year. The two biggest are the World Jiu-jitsu Championships (called the Mundials) and Abu Dhabi World Pro. These events allow the greatest grapplers in the world to show off their skills. You might be surprised to find that members of the Gracie family are still in the BJJ spotlight!

Brazilian jujitsu is a great way to get fit. It can help you make new friends. It's also an excellent form of self-defense, especially for smaller people. If this sounds like a good martial art for you, get in the dojo and start rolling!

GLOSSARY

commitment: A promise to do or give something.

competition: The act or process of trying to win a contest others are also trying to win. Also, the contest itself.

conserve: To prevent the waste of.

demonstration: An event staged to show people how something is used or done.

dominance: The state of being in control of or having more power than another.

flexibility: The ability to bend and stretch with ease.

frustrating: Causing feelings of disappointment and defeat.

hyperextend: To move a joint beyond its normal range of movement, risking injury.

opponent: Someone competing against another person.

spar: To practice a martial art with another person.

stamina: Strength that allows someone to continue doing something for a long period of time without getting tired.

submit: To give up.

technique: The manner in which physical movements are used for a particular purpose, such as training in a martial art.

INDEX

WEBSITES

Due to the changing nature of Internet links, PowerKids Press has developed an online list of websites related to the subject of this book. This site is updated regularly. Please use this link to access the list: www.powerkidslinks.com/ETD/BJJ